30 Years
of Publishing

Ontological Necessities

Also by Priscila Uppal

Ontological Necessities

PRISCILA UPPAL

Exile Editions

30 YEARS OF PUBLISHING

2006

Library and Archives Canada Cataloguing in Publication

Uppal, Priscila

Ontological necessities / Priscila Uppal.

Poems.

ISBN 1-55096-045-8

I. Title.

PS8591.P62O68 2006   C811'.54   C2006-903464-8

Design and Composition: Homonculous ReproSet
Typesetting: Moons of Jupiter
Printed in Canada: Gauvin Imprimerie

The publisher would like to acknowledge the financial assistance of
The Canada Council for the Arts.

 Conseil des Arts   Canada Council
du Canada   for the Arts

First published in Canada in 2006 by Exile Editions Ltd.
RR#1 Gen. Del.
144483 Southgate Road 14
Holstein, Ontario, N0G 2A0
info@exileeditions.com
www.ExileEditions.com

Sales Distribution:
McArthur & Company c/o Harper Collins
1995 Markham Road, Toronto, ON M1B 5M8
toll free: 1 800 387 0117   fax: 1 800 668 5788

for you, dear reader, my comrade, my bedfellow
my necessity

TABLE OF CONTENTS

III. MY MOTHER PRETENDS TO BE CHRIST

IV: THE WANDERER

What an accidental affair this living is after all our civilization.
—Virginia Woolf

I

NADJA, WHO ARE YOU?

Nadja, Who Are You?

are you the pencils that split at the apex
    of appointments

are you my father in a knit scarf
    off the plane, no meal to his name

are you winters in Ottawa
    sleigh bells on Parliament Hill & Francophone toffee

are you the glowing blue towels
    on the east side of swimmer's paradise

are you the chattering women with chattering teeth
    shuttled out on subway platforms

are you immensity and fragility and a cup of strong, orange tea
    teetering on a tightrope

are you the policeman with slips of pink paper in
    his robe pocket

are you the theatre bill, agit-props, white moustache of the director
    purple applause of the anemic

are you the sundial waitress in her two-bit automobile
    with a licence to fish

are you the aria, the apocryphal thunderstorm, the last lines
      of a dentist's speech to the comatose

are you the hydrogen light that flickers inside
          the lungs, hoards long intoxicating aerobic stretches of *ahhh*

are you the oyster shells of the new millennium
      upon meridian shores

are you a typewriter elegist, a black-keyed devotee
      in a dovetail coat

are you the wristwatch of the nation, little time
      for games, only gaming

are you the women's shelter of the soul, shifting through disasters
      and afternoon naps

are you the portrait-maker's stencil
      a cubed and cut valentine

are you the seventy-fifth Happy Birthday for a twenty-five-year-old
      cigar on the cake

are you the toadstool
      at the pondering

are you the wishing well
      at the christening

are you the cross-index battle waged on the longitudes of
        apprehension and illusion

are you the parties my mother wanted to attend
        in shocking red war-torn stockings

are you shocking red war-torn stockings, the kind that lick
        the thighs & festoon there, gluttonous

are you the shattered windowpanes
        of my virginity

the collapsed swings of
        anger

disastrous, you are
        I follow you across the etchings of another century

where men are not nearly
        as handsome

wives not nearly as
        understanding

where perception shifts like a sore
        collarbone and we writhe desperate

to readjust
keep kisses

on pillows

the nighttime prayers

the lamplights stutter

Who is this?

Who is this?

II

MONSTER

Don Quixote, You Sure Can Take One Helluva Beating

Don Quixote, you sure can take one
helluva beating! Even in this century, when windmills
turn to power plants and townships
into global trusts
             a head bruised to the shape of a basin
             a black eye smothered in curds
are sights still rare to behold indeed.

It's true, few children know of you, or can pronounce your name,
but just the same, those shiny shins
             and dislocated chins
             are to be admired
and they'd take a shot or two
             at your belly too
if you'd let 'em.

The rowdy renegades with car alarms
and stock market malaise, never embark on adventures
with their pants on,
             take back-to-nature
             back-to-basics retreats
seek pay dirt.

But first, to church, with roses and a hearse.
Your housekeeper and your niece rehearse;
the way is short, the singing worse:

errant knight
on your knees
of this life

I truly wish
we could circumvent
this fight

yet your fame
precedes you
and we undoubtedly
need you

to suffer the blows for every stupid dream we've ever had.

The End of the Paragraph

The heroine has informed her plot that she will escape. All of her things are in order: her adjectives have turned themselves in, nouns given up their residency cards, and the verbs, those precious little stones, are sewn smartly into her knickers. In the meantime she counts meal coupons and braids her hair into rope. Her lover asleep on the wrong exchange, she fantasizes he's singing medieval ballads on some old diesel train, but then must wash herself clean of that, must follow where the word leads, pull up her socks and adjust her jaunty cap, purse her lips against the electrical wires of our imagination and jump, jump, to the end of

Eighteen

When the monster was eighteen
she gave up smoking. Below the rock garden,
the buried remnants of her addiction

and the suspicion of a little extra stash
to screw the ecosystem. It was good
the shaking had ceased

fine to arrive at the realization of culpability
in the grand scheme of things. Love people,
hate others, leave notes in untidy places,
run over things in cars.

Surely, there was no place for her in this town, and yet,
she owned the pool hall, the hairdresser, the juvenile delinquency centre,
though she was the age of her peers, of her closest friends, of the boys
she'd sucked and fucked out of complacency.

A monster, but when she looked in the mirror,
the glass remained intact, did not crack. She applied
her lipstick one lip at a time. Men with hands
near their crotches didn't give her away
ordering three packs of cigarettes at the jukebox.

They waited for her to turn nineteen.
Then, you understand, they would really have some fun.

Poodle in the Painting

The poodle in the painting is a decoy.
Notice her perfectly curled fur,
her pillbox mane, her dark and beady eyes.

Think that behind the poodle
exists nothing: painting ceases
to derive any sort of meaning without the poodle.

If I told you that the poodle was not in fact a poodle
but only resembled a poodle because you cannot
fully picture death, would you believe me, or would
you find this whole adventure déclassé?

Never shot a poodle; but I will shoot
the poodle in this painting. We've not much
to say to each other and the night is very long.

Sorry, I Forgot to Clean Up After Myself

Sorry, Sirs and Madams, I forgot to clean up after myself
after the unfortunate incidents of the previous century.

How embarrassing; my apologies. I wouldn't advise you
to stroll around here without safety goggles, and I must insist
that you enter at your own risk. You may, however, leave
your umbrella at the door. Just keep your ticket.

We expected, of course, to have this all cleared away by the time
you arrived. The goal was to present you
with blue and green screens, whitewashed counters.

Unforeseen expenses.
Red tape.
So hard to find good help these days.

But, alas, excuses. Perhaps you will appreciate
the difficulties I've faced in providing you a clean slate.
If you step into a hole, Sirs and Madams, accept the loss
of a shoe or two. Stay the course.

Progress is the mother of invention. Here: take my hand.
Yes, that's right. You can return it on the way back.

Ontological Necessity

I'd like to bruise this earth
with mental missives until it cracks. If a volcano's brain
contains each eruption, we too must have these splits,
these dungeon pits inside us.

The harvest is nuclear.
My mouth, an octagon; my chest, an FBI file.
Stem cells grow off my neighbour's balcony, fall into my tea.
Cancer paid my tuition. On and on the hurricane
spies and trades. No one watches television
for the stories. Our universe is fresh out of those.
The galaxy yawns and pops pills.

Dear Self,
How am I to know if You are still alive?

Test me, you reply.

Bulgakov's Black Tom Cat Was Shot Several Times or
What We Can Look Forward to at the End of the War on Terror

The black tom who wreaked such havoc in Moscow
was shot several times by officers of the law
yet no bullets penetrated his skin (or fur, if you care to be exact).

The black tom enjoyed playing chess, a snifter of cognac,
pickled olives (sucked off a silver stick), and a ratty black tie.
A master of hypnosis (who could darn wool with astonishing speed),
to be sure, but a little lazy when it came to detailing the exposé.

For years now we've been asked to reconcile the end by the means,
the facts with the outcome, the effects to the cause.
And no one has come forward with an alternative.
The files were burned in any case (in whose case? his Master might ask).

Notwithstanding, the black tom hated to lose.
As he had throughout the century, he trusted the devil be with him.
He trusted no one would ask serious questions:
And he was right.

The Romantic Impulse Hits the Schoolyard

Wordsworth's daffodil heads hang
on the graffiti wall: *Go fuck your sister!*
the children call. Brakes jam,
                             cool kids take their pick,
now your precious ego is a piece of shit.
Partnered at recess, this is wrong,
the way balls thrown off
                             the roof is somehow wrong
in January, and how your precise steps
up the King-of-the-Castle walk compress
an avalanche beneath.
                        The lunch lady
shuffles the milk money. The sophomores play
murder ball and pray for revolution.
Endless preludes.
                        They'll be lucky if their teeth
are left intact,
if their brains don't suffer
a mild, or not so mild, concussion.

Never Held a Gun

Until noon hour the boy *never held a gun*
though German
he *never held a gun*

his mother claims he *never held a gun*
his father assures the media he *never held a gun*
his third-grade teacher confirms he *never held a gun*

The shrink writes:
A gun was never mentioned in any conversation.
When I said the word GUN he seemed not even to understand
that it is an object, perhaps just a noise
I made.

The police write:
From the gun we obtained nine sets of fingerprints; all belong
to the boy. He must have held the gun
a long time before deciding to fire.

Perhaps, one conjectures, he did not know how to hold it.
But he learned, learned quickly.

And would you look at the time?

Cheerleaders Sing of Genocide

Now that the lawns are empty and the school board shut down,
the cheerleaders (who stitch their *own* uniforms)
have regained creative control.

                           Legs at rest, tongues
perform acrobatics. Healthy girls
spring-load words: *Rah! Rah! Who's your daddy? Who's the best*
of the best of the best!
                    Songs flip-turn like valedictorians,
                    ride on tunes of body sculpting,
                    road rage, genocide.

Sally sticks her neck out for solar technology.
Tara cartwheels for a hypoallergenic tan.
After recess runners hook up to IVs.
Shopping carts toboggan back to homelands.

Now that the watering holes speak nonsense
and video games scour the ocean floor,
the cheerleaders sleep like slow sheep
who will soon be relegated to posture.

The Peculiar Deaths of Women Writers

From the executions of classically trained pornographers
to the acts of god (lightning, earthquakes, floods) that target
their homes, women writers die

before reaching forty, in childbirth or in bathrooms
while wringing out laundry, sorting socks and shirts or...

They take it well though, these ladies.
Their few lines in the recovery anthologies.
The patronizing critics who imagine
each a famous bard's sister in an alternate universe. Their bios
like thank-you notes for the invitation to the party.

I wake up with DT's when I think of all those women, winning
contests and giving up the prize, trying on
several pseudonyms for size, squatting
like dead ducks for gentleman callers
to make a strategic choice.

'Circumstances surrounding death unknown,' 'birth date an educated guess,'
details derived from diaries and letters from men which have survived:
a debt uncollected, friendship ended, a falling
out of favour with the court, destitute, prostitute,
hands tied behind backs and the barrels of shotguns.

At the National Exhibition we kill them four, five at a time.
That's me behind the decoys, between the plates. That's my grand prize
up for grabs. Time to take dictation:
I'm not going down without a fight
no matter how many fraternity boys come out tonight.

Samuel   Beckett
Adjusts   His Cap

Samuel   Beckett
        adjusts   his cap   and a nation explodes into   laughter,
making spectators a   little itchy.   I,   for one,   think it must
        be time   for   tea, but   our anthem   is
        playing   and   I must salute   for the sake of
our people   who are   returning from   the wars of the   past
into   the wars   of   the present with   more gods
        than cigarettes   in their backpacks   and   more cartoons
than heartache   upon   their   peace-keeping   lips.

Tolstoy, Unrecognized

Let us forget the scores of women holding themselves up
at night scratching at their scalps in agony: *Why, why,*
couldn't Vronsky be kinder?

Let us forget the boy and the little girl too (underdeveloped
brats in the end). We know children
stand in the way of love, which is why
they begin in our bellies.

I'm not going to deny that Tolstoy is Russian
and Russian novels are worth reading:
the excruciating attention to the soul,
unspoken tortures running amok between the sexes.
All these predicaments are well handled.

Anna knew the train schedules,
a trait to be admired in a heroine.
But she did not know her own heart.

Neither did Leo.
The tome is no masterpiece on love and its discontents.
Pick it up again, dear reader. Your youth made you forget:

It's a treatise on farming:
at close the ones who survive concentrate
human effort on the land.
The women in tears put their trust in man.

My Ovidian Education

After a long respite in the lavatory trying to get my head around
how so many twenty-somethings and a few older ladies
can think of nothing better to say after a presentation on Paul Celan
than "That was deep I guess, was this guy gay?"
I emerge with a blazer as white as chalk dust
and a pencil case as dour as a coffin and leaning into the mirror
discover I have aggravatingly beautiful cheeks and deep-set
Firestone tire eyes but a nose with a hook as sharp
as the old hermit in my Renaissance plates dictionary. Under
the neon lights of the chemistry hallway, eating an orange,
a banana, and a box of SunMaid raisins, I would sell my soul
for a student worth Platonizing about and a stack of letters
urging me to adulterize my standards just this once
and leave them all sitting there without a second act after intermission
to their exercices on metaphor and lists of ten questions
to ask of their poems, including "Why should anyone but you
care about what you've written?" and dive off the top
of academe's steeple cracking my nose on the concrete
waiting for the one with the shiniest apple to sing me and Paul back to life.

What Johnny **Won't** *Read*

Shakespeare or *Waiting for Godot,*
War and Peace, Daniel Defoe
An Introduction to Abnormal Psychology 101
The instructions on shampoo
The terms and conditions of his Mastercard
Movie subtitles, Chinese menus,
Letters to the Editor, the calendar

Passport guidelines, Christmas cards
Internet text longer than his fingers
Parking passes, blueprints
Excerpts from the 9/11 Commission
Jehovah's Witness pamphlets, side effects stickers
Why Johnny Can't Read
Articles in *Playboy*

The Charter of Rights and Freedoms
Divorce papers and minds
His father's suicide note
STOP signs
This

Women Don't Write Manifestos

History will testify: we were never good communists.
Let's not be comrades. I'm not your leader.
Just give me a fair price for my wares.
And one day, when the wind blows the other way,
you can commandeer my children,
all nine of them, if you must.

I have few fresh theories to purport,
avant-garde advice.
I won't insist one colour
is more beautiful than another.

What do I care?
I must live off-colour.
I must live.

Elegy for a Deadbeat Dad

Don't come around here no more. Write that
on my tombstone. Keep your flowers. They give
me the willies, and I've got too many shakes
as it is. Recite a limerick, not a prayer.
It's a joke here. Give your old man
the luxury of a joke now and then. I never
put much faith in ceremony.

Remember when your mother took the hamper of money?
You don't. I guess that was before your time. She had a sense of humour,
then, that woman was wild, believe it or not. She clipped each crisp bill
to the clothesline until they flew away. I called them fighter pigeons, after,
of course, after I calmed down. Your mother said once you were old enough
to understand, you too wouldn't want no dirty business in the house. She still
let me touch her once or twice after that, but the writing was on the wall
and it spoke like my own mother, and I had no need for two.
I hope we can agree that no one needs two.

And as for fathers, I guess no one needs two of those either. Stepkids.
You heard about them I bet. They're ok, I guess. Probably'll stop by
with cheese and crackers or a pie or something. I wish I could be buried in
a cigar box. Tell the minister that's my wish. That kind of thing.

The freaky thing about living is that it goes on while you're busy trying to beat it.
I had a perfect cribbage hand once, framed and hung it in the kitchen.
No one ever dared move it, but I guess some asshole at the Sally Ann

is going to drive away with it in his back seat for a buck or two.
I wanted to give it to you.

This is no time, I suppose, to dwell on what we can't do.
I hear you're a good kid. You shacked up with some nice woman.
Hope it works out. You should have a couple of kids, too,
just to see what it's about.

Now, take your old man down to the corner. I'm tired and hungry,
and this town's got no clock and no women
to distract us.

Let's get polluted.
Whadda ya say?

Romance

The scientist secures a wife at the convention.
She smiles: husbands are successful inventions.
Elevators arrive, transporting love to another dimension.

If you want a baby, he says, *spit on my hand*.
She gladly sheds her scarves and gives commands.
The scientist secures a wife at the convention.

Give me a new chart, he demands from reception.
I will never forget you, she replies, firm in her selection.
Elevators arrive, transporting love to another dimension.

When the child speaks, what will they tell him?
When the child hears, what will they mention?
The scientist needs a new wife to attend a convention.

He'll grow free of all this nonsense about evolution.
She'll be pleased with her own sense of circumvention.
The child will trap love in a single dimension.

At the end of the day, scientists begin in test tubes.
At the end of the world, wives close the vestibules.
The location changes, but it's the same convention.
Love elevates and plummets, and we affirm known dimensions.

Summer Escape

Children, their hands upon desks.
Palms down, flat, knuckles ready for rapping.

Teacher takes out her pointer and her hairpins.
The clock has already struck *summer* but the long lines
of cursive have yet to surrender.

We are not of this time, says the girl in the front row.
The children gasp. Teacher insists upon silence.
A few pads twitch.

If I brought you my life you'd know what time it is,
Teacher replies, produces an apple, twirls
and throws it up like a coin.

I dare you, says the boy, the one with the multiplication tables
on the inside of his elbows, planet roll call
underneath his five-ring binder.

Yes, comes the answer. *Yes, you do.*
When out of the wardrobe springs an old woman, a mattress,
a ticket stub, and a fence.

The children begin building. The boy and the girl
rush down to the gymnasium,
Teacher steps behind them.

They play with her life until the janitors turn out the lights.

Grabbing Summer by His Throat

No interest in winter's afterthoughts, let's cover our ears,
stamp our feet, shake the sleet and rain and defeat
out of our hair for an hour or two (come on
sunrise, don't dick us around, the strata of our longing
have shifted under cement long enough).

I've purchased my ticket and you've promised me a ride.
The whole gang's here and we'll act like we've got plenty of time.
But you've got our number, and we've got yours
(step into my office for just a moment
and soon I think we will both see eye to eye).

Hang the sun by the collar, hoping it won't wet its pants.
These are the don't-fuck-with-me months.

The moon plunks a coin into a handbasket.
Two months' stay in hell, he will return a new man.
And you, my friend, will barely recognize him.
All it takes is one season to strain the old friendship.

The Fountain

Thirsty? Drink up.
The rules are simple. Like fish, you flit to the shores
of my lips and we kiss, we kiss

like lepers. Tongue, neck, trusting head
loll. Shoulders shrug out of existence. Eyes
capsize, drown as you dwindle.

Turn back? Then we'll turn back, to the first broken cell,
iniquity of prime conception. Like the apple
at the core, I feed off every second

you live. I spit back seeds.
Unpleased, you invent dreaming, invent youth
as if you are a firefly whose electricity

is your one attribute, as if you have no intention
of dying at all. Wouldn't it be safer to just stay put?
But you refuse sound advice,

well-intentioned advances. And I wash
your sad skin like some old Halloween costume.
And you scare dried plants. And only straw dogs knock at your door.

Displaced Matter iIs Another Term for Dirt

Stand by the house you built like a cake from scratch.
Peel secrets off the wall's skin and

swallow.

Hack a friendship. File a litmus test on the forehead of Mars.
Take a mouthful into the flu-jaws of the nation.

Cough.

Sniff the aborted mission of your own osmosis. Forgive
the aching jukebox. Elders do not ask for

visits.

Immigration outdates pilgrimage.

Cleaning the Piano

It was a fun party, a martini party, and people drank.
They drank a lot.

Duck paté flew over the hibiscus.
Toilet paper landed on the deck.
Brie latched onto the hostess' smile,
laughter contagious all the while.

It was the sort of party where people sing songs
and even those who don't know the words
hum the tune. And neighbours stop fucking each other
over and just start fucking. It was the sort of party
where the police drop by for punch.
Oh yes, it will be on the minds
of its guests for years to come, maybe generations.

Why must our host clean the piano?
Um, the entire guest list ended up, well—
the music so grand they had to *get inside*.
One woman's whole childhood was
in that damn song. One man uncovered
his abandoned mother. The teacher, her orgasm.
The doctor, her self-esteem.

It was a messy party. The kind that leaks
into your morning like an endless whistle;
you don't know why it hurts so much
when you wash, when you think.

And no one can quite figure out how the music started.
The piano is hollow.
No strings. No keys.

And maybe in the end we even mouthed the words.

No Angels in This Death Poem

Absolutely no angels in this death poem.
Half-baked poets offer angels for consolation
the way neighbours offer fruitcake at Christmas.

Absolutely no talk of Christmas in this death poem.
Resurrection went out with yesterday's trash and
holy stars and wise men appear on hockey jerseys.

Absolutely no wise men in this death poem.
Wise men have never made dying understandable.
They've drawn no pie charts or graphs for the soul.

Absolutely no mention of souls in this death poem.
The soul is not a ship, or a bird, or a flag, or a flower.
We have no power of attorney over it, no death connection.

Absolutely no mention of death in this death poem.
Angels are listening and the wise men are sketching.
Look at where all these souls are headed and tell no one.

Film Version of My Hatred

Opening scene: music mute, the visual aid
of a hand, gloved in white, suffocates the dawn
that dares to reappear. Coffee brews, zoom percolator,
an aroma penetrates numb nostrils, tastes bitter,
muddy, and my hate coughs until something hard and brown
is dislodged. Dialogue: heads covered in paper bags:

What you got against wonder?

My lap was stung by a thousand bees.

Liar.

*Can't you see the way those assholes
are looking at me?
Can't you hear the fucking hissing?
What am I supposed to do with all that?*

You could love it.

I could. But no.

Red. Flash. Lists of unknown actors.
Kaboom!   and   *Aha!*
in blue.

Someone will attempt to hold the frame with brittle arms.
A woman most likely, a single fan who hasn't yet lost hope,
thinks the movie worth making

sans budget and producer. My heart will be played
by my worst enemy, my thoughts by conflicting weather patterns.
I end only if the audience participates.

Outrage

Five bottles of milk on the counter.
None priced.

Your mother in the dairy aisle
pleading with her eggs.

Fortune Cookies on the Other Side of the World

*If you say your lover's name seven times over the course of seven seconds
you will grow tired of your lover even sooner than expected.*

❦

*If a cat scratches against your pant leg in the late evening,
let him sleep beside you. For your warmth, he will offer you
nothing in return, and that is a good lesson.*

❦

*Pin a flower to your lapel at the start of every work week.
Name each one.
When you start running out, you will understand how god feels.*

❦

Martyr Complex

I died one morning.
Next morning I died again.
Following morning I died one more time.

In the interim I learned
I earned several million followers.
My face now legendary.
The white lights of cities and country villages
spelt my name.

I died one more time.
In this instance I broke apart
like a giant piñata, guts spilled everywhere
over all my followers
in the cities and country villages
obscuring my name.

I turned away one last time.
My eyes stuck on the highest mountain.
I watched the world die.
I watch it now and again every morning.

To the One Who Set All This in Motion

We refuse to surrender. Watch the woman
on the corner buying biscuits with her child.
She has weighed them carefully against her
rent and newspaper, holds out for
week-old fruit tossed in a bin outside.

He refuses to surrender. Will continue
to empty his bed pan all the days
of his life, take his medicines and
spit in your face, trace the memories
he's got left with the vengeance
of a man determined to resuscitate.

The animals too refuse. Form secret
societies, breed willingly and openly
with other species. Thumbs grow from
paws, spines from gills, pits off skin.
They stormtroop underground.

You may have been the one who
set all this in motion, but I too refuse
to let up until you strike me down
for all eternity. We curse You.
You can have none of it, even less than we.

The Poem Can Be Completed by Anyone

This is difficult for me to admit, but the poem
can be completed by anyone. You need not invest any particular
time or money into it; you need not even care much
for the results, the eventual outcome, as long as you lend your ear
for an instant, we will deem the experiment complete,
and you can be on your way, contemplate how it is you ended up
with those brats for children, this county for your namesake,
when you had ideals once, dreams, and you even used to pick up
a book or two, not that you ever thought much about poets,
but they were ok, worth keeping around, and so it might come to you
as a surprise but this poem needs you, whoever you are, it doesn't really
matter as long as you have eyes, as long as you breathe, whether
it's into the air or by tube, makes no difference, but you must
have at least the faintest pulse, a poem needs at least that to go on,
though it need not be finished, it's had so much trouble finishing lately,
what with everything else and all, which is why, poor passersby,
I've latched onto you the business of seeing this one through:
What is it you'd like to say?
What do you have to say for yourself?

Monster

Under the bed, I wait for you to drop your book.
One by one I will eat the pages, every word,
until I grow fat on your illiteracy, then
slither like an unvoiced question out the door.

III

MY MOTHER PRETENDS TO BE CHRIST

On the Psychology of Crying Over Spilt Milk

According to Freud's observations and analysis of his nephew fantasy-making with a shoe, the *fort-da* game is the necessary foundational basis by which a child can rightfully count on a parent who leaves for work or an office party or a trip to the Bahamas with her younger lover to eventually return.

The child, controlling the outcome, sees that through simple will and aggression he can force the shoe to go, then facilitate retrieval whenever he so desires. This, according to Freud, makes it easier for the child to accept separation of all kinds. *Fort-da* is *mourning play*.

Hence, in tragedies, shoes play important roles. Actors must think carefully about where to step. Frequently, prints are drawn in light chalk on the stage. No one likes to share a pair. Letters are pulled from their lips, as are knives. When boots find their mark, victims claim the soles.

Children must be encouraged to play *fort-da*. Freud said so, and he had very healthy relationships. For those of you whose parents have left and never returned, you happen to be screwed, psychologically speaking. Perhaps, as in the most successful tragedies, you should seek revenge.

This House Has No Doorbell

You arrive with all your luggage (didn't your parents
teach you manners?), your business card and a letter from
your distant aunt *Darling, let's see how much you've grown.*

But this house has no identifiable number and the flowerpots
hide no keys. Around back a cat without a collar
struts on a glider, licks mouse bones.

You check your watch and discover time
an outdated concept. Your map folds itself into a bird.
Fly, fly back to childhood it cries.

But you see through those lies. Your joints are ancient
and the roof of the house is like a propeller
rising you into age, experience, and unflinching, uncompromising death.

Shuffling on the porch, you've prepared your speech so thoroughly:
I used to live here, would you mind terribly
if I looked around?

But this house has no doorbell, no knocker, no windows to peer inside.
And you are as old as your childhood.
And eternity rests out the back.

That Presupposes One Has an Individual Nervous System

The anxiety attacks stem from my mother's side (the one with the long lists
     of psychiatric units)

my long fingers extend from that branch too, my great-grandmother a pianist,
     great-grandfather a composer

my father ingratiated a mind for mathematics, hairy legs, hiccups
     and the desire to pull my toenails out every New Year's Eve

I don't know who my uncle is, and my aunts are all footnotes, never met them, not once,
     but I shudder from something stuttering around inside
     and I'm sure they must resent it as much as I

Lunch Note

It has come to my attention *Lunch is the most important meal of the day.* The nurse was very firm on this point after I was lifted from the floor. Don't be mad—my dress was not soiled and I was able to retie the sash without too much trouble once feeling in my fingers returned. It was a bit scary though to see the other kids' faces around me—especially Jessica's because she's usually so nice and I knew that I must look weird for her to be staring so rudely. I think Marlene was even crying, but she's always crying so it's difficult to tell if she was looking my way or not. Mrs. Henning *had it up to here* with the Geography lesson. The boys kept snickering when she'd say *Hungary*. I don't know why, since it makes me sad to say the word *Hungary*. I could see the millions of people she told us lived there in *Budapest* starving and being so used to it that they didn't know they were starving. Now those kids need help. I think that's where our Halloween *UNICEF* money goes, but I'm not sure. I don't know what lots of Canadian pennies buys. But I hope it buys lunch. The nurse was pretty nice in the end. She told me to forget the rest of the lesson and have a glass of orange juice and three Oreo cookies. You packed me those cookies, Mom, and I thank you. You are always thinking of treats and I got a great big bag! It's just that the nurse says I should have a sandwich or something or crackers and cheese. I'm sure you know best though. I mean the other kids, even Brandon and Percy, they're always trying to trade for mine. But I know you wouldn't like that so I always refuse. The nurse gets paid to say stuff like that about lunch. Like Mrs. Henning who gets paid to say *Hungary*. And the boys laugh. But they laugh at a lot. Though they stopped laughing when I was lifted from the floor.

Mother Bought a Plane Ticket

She packed the passports
and all our clothes.

Father said she even took
the windows, though he must have stared
through something.

I ran the tap, said,
She took all the water
too.

Now what are we
going to do?

Mother bought a plane ticket
so we stood
on the lawn with our
signs and waved.

Three years ago
something like a woman
fell into my hands.

Her Organs Were Drying Up

Over the years father told me that several men in white suits
brought babies to my mother. He used the term *swaddled*
and so I took his word for it.

The white suits gleamed in the moonlight, which father
insisted was providence. I've never understood
providence although I've looked it up
on at least five different occasions.

My mother was on her knees in the garden
sucking on blueberries, but father felt
it wise to leave out such unimportant details.
An apple or *a peach* and what would have been different?

I opened my mouth and *Good God!* came out.
My father was worried I'd end up religious.
My mother was merely worried.

Several men in white suits stood in the shadows
with buckets and buckets of water and children trapped
in flowerpots singing *We are the glory of the earth*.

Motorcycle Accidents
and Other Things That Remind Me of Mother

wigs on fake white heads in the flashy store window
the sound of chattering teeth after heaving out of the lake onto stones
smell of cranberry sauce simmering on the stove before Thanksgiving
you travel in waves, mother,
                like a drowning sweater in November

boys in overalls beating buckets with dolls
the sunflower in my orthodontist's office
snails in thick white cream at the Bistro
the bruise on my inner thigh father insists on calling a beauty mark
I heard you once
              on the radio
singing along with Carmen Miranda
but I wasn't reminded

the beaks of geese wrangling a plastic shopping bag for crumbs
my lover's back when I step on it
eight-week-old celery after it has gone sticky and white
and I must throw it out or stomach the hard water
              the instant coffee maker
gurgles and spits
              you remind me of it
turn off when unused

petunias on high windowsills
purple velvet gloves in an older woman's purse
the head of a vole the cat brought home

Emergency Broadcast System's messages

                              burnt bagels
ham sandwiches on rye
                         in picnic baskets
out of season
                         mother, we clash
                         making room on the grass

the unhurt fender of a truck by the back-bent leg
a siren since gone mute with fistfuls of forms
my disgust upon seeing the lip of some bastard's shoe embedded in the road

Purse

Large on purpose, my mother's purse hangs by her side
like a colostomy bag. She is a suffering woman,
and her organs know it.

Streets have the nerve to exist when she walks upon them,
clouds have the hubris to puff, the *caju* trees know
how to bleed such sonorous juice that her ears
burn in discomfort.

Flowers turn like pinwheels inside her mind.
Her children scurry like mice.
If she zips open her purse, be advised:
Her memories are having seizures.

The whole thing might spill out.
Then she'd really be a target for the pickpockets.

I'm Afraid of Brazilians **or** *Visiting the Ancestral Homeland*
Is Not the Great Ethnic Experience Promised by Other Memoirs

Against all political correctness,
I must say it,
I must admit:
I'm afraid of Brazilians.

I don't like them.
I don't like this country.
I don't like this language.
I don't even like this currency.

And not in the mystical sense.
Or the abstract.
Or the perfectly hypothetical.

I can't blame this fear
on movies, or television programming,
or the front covers
of *Time* magazine.
No.

I'm afraid of Brazilians.
I am visiting Brazil
(my mother's country)
and I'm afraid, truly afraid
of every Brazilian I meet.

This is not something you can say
in a poem, you tell me.
Please don't compose this poem
here: in broad daylight
where any self-respecting Brazilian
could feel perfectly justified
peeking over your shoulder
to see what you've written.

Please, not so loud, you say.
You haven't given them a chance.

You're right, I admit.
(I can certainly admit it.)
I've given them no chance
to please me. Don't you

understand, this is the nature
of being afraid, and this is
the nature of the poem
I am writing, which must
get written, no matter
what the climate

or the reception
(here, in my mother's country
or abroad
or in my own ears).

Decorating, My Father

strung up paper links in purple and blue
bells cut out of tissue
angels with the hair pencilled in

the festive memories hang
as coffee is served
with a shot of rum
and presents are opened
that no one needs

this season
we fight three times
out of three
(why can't you just listen for once—
that was ten years ago—
stop harping on the past—
stop bringing up

how I've failed
again) the ticket
costing a little more
than we'd planned
wishing we'd
asked to stay over
at a friend's

yet this is his pride:
not the words or the books
or the photograph
in the paper
a launch in New York

my childhood decorations
made by unskilled hands
fingers red from scissors
eyes red from crying
thinking it won't be fine enough
to please

these are alive
as the resurrection

the black hairs on your arms
unbearable
as the cold

your chest
stuffed and failing
(I'm old—my heart could stop
at any second—why
kill an old man)

and I'm unskilled
again, no poem to offer you
no fine dedication
that will turn your head

I unwrap
a brand new calendar
and expound
upon the Munch exhibit
at the gallery

when all you want
are paper angels in gold dresses
and holly ripped
out of a magazine
on the walls

the words
from a daughter
that could shatter the world's ice
on Xmas morning:

Ball,
Dadda,
Luv.

The Missing Link and Father

In an algebraic equation my father would be X
though he wouldn't mark a spot
or cross anything out
or represent the locked box of a century's old mystery.

Instead, I would keep him (if I could)
in the left pocket of my lover's trousers
and I'd wait months for a special occasion
for him to be found. "Well, what do you know?"
I can hear my lover say. "What do you know?"

My father would like to be surprised, I think,
like a twenty-dollar bill or a stash of subway
tokens. No one's looked at him as a small
forgotten treasure in some time. I'd like to
tack him to a bulletin board, highlighted
in yellow, or clip him to the refrigerator.

I've been following the red arrows
and the short, paradoxical clues. Father, I'm on to you.
There may not be a huge surprise on the other side,
but I promise to yell (yell your name) real loud.

Father's Wheelchair Is Purchased by the Smithsonian

The tall men weren't necessary. We all said so.
Nominated by the triumvirate keepers of historical destiny,
my father acquiesced the artifact with little fuss.

When they hoisted him up, he made only a slight whimper,
the kind of noise that should be blamed upon reflex
rather than resistance, and his eyeglasses fell to the floor

from the force of gravity. My father is cooperative.
All his papers are in order, and he would have been happy to donate
his chair to the authorities, no deal was necessary.

Not that we destroyed the documents, on the contrary, we kept them.
My father's sheets are stuffed with duplicates. Without the vehicle
and since our arms are easily exhausted, he spends

much more time in bed than he used to, but old habits die hard.
Every spoon needs a fork! Every sun needs a moon!
Poor wheelchair, he cries, *you're empty without me!*

It is truly debatable what you *should* or *should not* have taken
that day. The deal we struck was for the wheelchair
and the wheelchair only (as the object which most represented

my father in his time). Every day, other things go missing.
First his shirts, then socks, then teeth. I can't wait
for the exhibit to open (they keep promising *soon soon*)

so all of us who love him can climb up on his chair again.
So my brother can go back to patrolling the neighbourhood.
So my mother can resume that nasty business of having children.

My Mother Pretends to Be Christ

She says it is a trick of every woman
to attract a man by sitting alone in the square,
aloof (in some circumstances even
genuinely suffering), filing her nails.

Common Book Pillow Book

Long enough since the genre was popular
we've forgotten what to call it: weird mix of quotes and collectibles, private
thoughts and uncensored meditations in brief, like locks of hair and
child height charts of your considerations
and ponderings. An abandoned art, you practise it with care: each quote
equal to the other, simple entries like coordinates of unmarked appearances
in the sky—twenty years, over
8,000 days—the weather is "what you make of sunshine," and only women "can
make a man successful," haven't you heard
"God is the messenger, and we are all brothers and sisters," organizations
of hate "must be fought with the ultimate crest: humanity," and you
note a quote with a love reserved
for precision and the unattained, and I
suspend like cracked meteors in the ether
of your common message: go to bed, what is truly important in this world
has already been said.

"When people deserve love the least
is when they need it the most," we are the axis
of cliché, "like mother like daughter," sign your name
on this one before I turn out the light
and resume my interrupted prayer.

Father, the Odds Are I Will Not Be There When You Die

So take this poem as a token of my appreciation
for all the things you did that fathers are supposed to do
and all the things you couldn't do too.

I know it will be hard, and painful,
disorienting, unbearably lonely.
And I know you will tell your friends
and nurses that your daughter is a very
successful, busy, modern woman;
a house, a husband, duties of her own.
And I know you will mean it too.
So let me say thank you, again.

But the truth is, I don't want to be
by your side when the time comes
though I might actually bring you solace
and help you pass the time.

The world is a cruel place. You told me so, often.
I've banked my life on this verity.
So take this poem as a token of my appreciation.
May it spawn more grateful progeny than me.

Survey: What Have You Learned From Dying?

–It doesn't last long.

–You can't prepare enough for the end.

–Those beside your bed are those that deserve forgiveness.

–I would have had children.

–Everything I used to hold dear—the rain, air, snow—
  are now enemies.

–Birthdays and anniversary parties are worth every single penny.
  Have one each day for the sun.

–I would have spent more summers at home.

–I wouldn't have worried so much about my weight.

–There is nothing to fear once you give in, hold up your hands and yell:
  You damn bastard—I recognize you there in the dark!

–You suffer ten times more than you ever let on.

–Flowers are uninspired gifts.

–God knows me.

–There is no God.

–A scream is more genuine than all the prayers in heaven.

–Silence is not golden.

Three Cats Guard This House

One at each entrance, their duty
to protect.

          We may not own much,
but what we do, we'd like to keep.

The cats lick their paws.
The cats fight.
The cats sanitize their wounds.

You see, I let them think there is only one cat
in the house. It's a security issue.
Keeps them on their toes.

A cat without an enemy is like a cat without a meow.

Now, get your head out of my dish
before the three cats spot you.

The house belongs to one of them.
When the pouncing begins, try to determine
if you can guess which.

Insurgence

Pinch her breast and it will swell into Armageddon.

IV

THE WANDERER

The Wanderer: A New Millennium Translation

The individual always waits
for prosperity, for favours of state although he is troubled at heart
and monitors the ice-cold waters with bare
hands, and surfs the tangled airwaves
the path of an interloper. The state is relentless!

So the wanderer says, traumatized by hardships,
the cruelties of crossfires, the deaths of once-dear neighbours.
"I wake alone, each and every morning.
No one lives here anymore.
I confess only to myself:
I know
it should be a responsible citizen's
practice to firmly constrict the chest,
keep it air-tight and closed, no matter what one thinks.
For cynical minds cannot withstand the state
or help protect unstable consciences.
Eager for glories, these troubled minds
must remain sane.
So I should command my own head
depressed and doped, worried and wanting,
deprived of my country, far from my people.

It's been years since we buried our leader
in the soil's zero and I've travelled
spent and saggy, misguided as the wind,
seeking someone who will take me in, bring

me back to some vibrant place, the city's squares, where I might
find news, someone might remember
the old name of my country, my people, offer me a room,
a meal, remind me what these things used to mean.

For those who want to put themselves in my shoes,
an individual without compatriots, know that the path
of an interloper is no path at all,
it is dirty money, frozen faces, far, far
from human luxury.
For those who want to put themselves in my shoes,
think about the costs! Who pays the bill?
For those who want to put themselves in my shoes,
know that you must deny all the intellectuals' warnings
for our time, know that drugs and sleep
steer the individual's will—in his mind
he lies still in his lover's arms,
on top of the world
his nation's flag resting on his gun
as before.

But then one wakes a leaderless man
who sees before him the shallow waves
the pigeons wandering, grey feathers tarnishing
rain, sleet, snow, and hail.
Then the fat belly, sore from stealing
and concealing, is suddenly silent as
the mind passes back through memory, where old friends
are greeted genuinely and eagerly, and there is time
for everything. But they drift out of reach. They drown.

Pigeons sing the same damn songs. Despair hijacks
the anxious, beaten heart.
So it's baffling, it's uncouth, but my heart is still here.
It hasn't disappeared. When I think of all my old neighbours,
how they slipped through the cracks,
or those young brash misinformed soldiers. This is life then—
every day declines and falls and no one
knows a thing who hasn't lived through
his share of governments. To survive, you must be patient,
must keep your plans secret, trust no one, know when
to press the button and when to head underground. Do not
fear, do not take so much that others notice, do not act too cocky
before you've assessed all the players.

A winner waits before claiming victory
to predict exactly how the populace will act—must thoroughly understand
how disastrous it will be when all the world's
resources are wasted, all the world's towers blown to bits,
all the bays bombed, and in every civic hall and private home,
all the people lie dead.

We die stupid and scared at the wall.
And war destroys everyone, carries each nation back
to the past in a bird's beak over turbulent waters.
The bald eagle claws the once-innocent child
fugitive in a grave.

Yes, we destroyed this city.
We destroyed laughter. We destroyed tears.
So long, suckers. So long.

And you, who put yourself in these shoes,
think hard about this—no one grows old anymore.
Who can remember how this slaughter started? No one asks:
Where have all the houses gone?
Where have all the youth gone?
Where have all the gods gone?
Who enjoys this night's feast?
Who sits pretty in the hall?

Oh fucking bastard! Oh fucking shit!
Go fuck yourself and your fucking freedom! Times haven't changed
under the cover of your new night—nothing new exists. Nothing.

On the border stand our old allies,
captive by fantastic fireworks in the skies. There they go now—Poof!
What's left but ash? What's left
but weapons and greed and the glorious state.
What's left but videos and cellphones and eternal terror?
What's left for soldiers but suicide?

In the new millennium, be on high alert.
Every operation shatters heaven.
This is no place for friends.
This is no place for leaders.
This is no place for bodies.
This is no place for man.
Our ownership papers are forged."

So says anyone who is half-awake, sort-of listening.
Freedom is for believers, for those who won't cry,

for the one who says, yes, I am a defender of all that is good,
and an enemy to all that is evil.
Have courage.
Freedom begs for mercy,
suffering fortune with the strong,
with those who promise eternal protection.

To a Future Reader

I beg you, tell me
the words I left
ended up funny,
gave you guffaws
as the planet
went all to hell
in ways I was not
sad enough to imagine.

Ave Atque Vale
Farewell

Notes

The Wanderer: A New Millennium Translation is an extremely liberal post 9/11 translation of the Old English poem-elegy "The Wanderer" (Exeter Book, circa 975 AD). The following is the standard edition of "The Wanderer" as printed in *The Anglo-Saxon Poetic Records Vol III: The Exeter Book* edited by George Philip Krapp and Elliot Van Kirk Dobbie (Columbia University Press, 1936). Special thanks to Columbia University Press for permission to reprint the poem.

THE WANDERER

Oft him anhaga   are gebideð,
metudes miltse,   þeah þe he modcearig
geond lagulade   longe sceolde
hreran mid hondum   hrimcealde sæ,
5 wadan wræclastas.   Wyrd bið ful aræd!
    Swa cwæð eardstapa,   earfeþa gemyndig,
wraþra wælsleahta,   winemæga hryre:
"Oft ic sceolde ana   uhtna gehwylce
mine ceare cwiþan.   Nis nu cwicra nan
10 þe ic him modsefan   minne durre
sweotule asecgan.   Ic to soþe wat
þæt biþ in eorle   indryhten þeaw,
þæt he his ferðlocan   fæste binde,
healde his hordcofan,   hycge swa he wille.
15 Ne mæg werig mod   wyrde wiðstondan,
ne se hreo hyge   helpe gefremman.
Forðon domgeorne   dreorigne oft
in hyra breostcofan   bindað fæste;
swa ic modsefan   minne sceolde,
20 oft earmcearig,   eðle bidæled,
freomægum feor   feterum sælan,
siþþan geara iu   goldwine minne
hrusan heolstre biwrah,   ond ic hean þonan
wod wintercearig   ofer waþema gebind,

25 sohte sele dreorig   sinces bryttan,
   hwær ic feor oþþe neah   findan meahte
   þone þe in meoduhealle   min mine wisse,
   oþþe mec freondleasne   frefran wolde,
   weman mid wynnum.   Wat se þe cunnað,
30 hu sliþen bið   sorg to geferan,
   þam þe him lyt hafað   leofra geholena.
   Warað hine wræclast,   nales wunden gold,
   ferðloca freorig,   nalæs foldan blæd.
   Gemon he selesecgas   ond sincþege,
35 hu hine on geoguðe   his goldwine
   wenede to wiste.   Wyn eal gedreas!
      Forþon wat se þe sceal   his winedryhtnes
   leofes larcwidum   longe forþolian,
   ðonne sorg ond slæp   somod ætgædre
40 earmne anhogan   oft gebindað.
   Þinceð him on mode   þæt he his mondryhten
   clyppe ond cysse,   ond on cneo lecge
   honda ond heafod,   swa he hwilum ær
   in geardagum   giefstolas breac.
45 Ðonne onwæcneð eft   wineleas guma,
   gesihð him biforan   fealwe wegas,
   baþian brimfuglas,   brædan feþra,
   hreosan hrim ond snaw,   hagle gemenged.
      Þonne beoð þy hefigran   heortan benne,
50 sare æfter swæsne.   Sorg bið geniwad,
   þonne maga gemynd   mod geondhweorfeð;
   greteð gliwstafum,   georne geondsceawað
   secga geseldan.   Swimmað eft on weg!
   Fleotendra ferð   no þær fela bringeð
55 cuðra cwidegiedda.   Cearo bið geniwad
   þam þe sendan sceal   swiþe geneahhe
   ofer waþema gebind   werigne sefan.
      Forþon ic geþencan ne mæg   geond þas woruld
   for hwan modsefa   min ne gesweorce,

60 þonne ic eorla lif   eal geondþence,
   hu hi færlice   flet ofgeafon,
   modge maguþegnas.   Swa þes middangeard
   ealra dogra gehwam   dreoseð ond fealleþ,
   forþon ne mæg weorþan wis   wer, ær he age
65 wintra dæl in woruldrice.   Wita sceal geþyldig,
   ne sceal no to hatheort   ne to hrædwyrde,
   ne to wac wiga   ne to wanhydig,
   ne to forht ne to fægen,   ne to feohgifre
   ne næfre gielpes to georn,   ær he geare cunne.
70 Beorn sceal gebidan,   þonne he beot spriceð,
   oþþæt collenferð   cunne gearwe
   hwider hreþra gehygd   hweorfan wille.
   Ongietan sceal gleaw hæle   hu gæstlic bið,
   þonne ealre þisse worulde wela   weste stondeð,
75 swa nu missenlice   geond þisne middangeard
   winde biwaune   weallas stondaþ,
   hrime bihrorene,   hryðge þa ederas.
   Woriað þa winsalo,   waldend licgað
   dreame bidrorene,   duguþ eal gecrong,
80 wlonc bi wealle.   Sume wig fornom,
   ferede in forðwege,   sumne fugel oþbær
   ofer heanne holm,   sumne se hara wulf
   deaðe gedælde,   sumne dreorighleor
   in eorðscræfe   eorl gehydde.
85 Yþde swa þisne eardgeard   ælda scyppend
   oþþæt burgwara   breahtma lease
   eald enta geweorc   idlu stodon.
       Se þonne þisne wealsteal   wise geþohte
   ond þis deorce lif   deope geondþenceð,
90 frod in ferðe,   feor oft gemon
   wælsleahta worn,   ond þas word acwið:
   "Hwær cwom mearg?   Hwær cwom mago?   Hwær cw
                                maþþumgyfa?
   Hwær cwom symbla gesetu?   Hwær sindon seledream
   Eala beorht bune!   Eala byrnwiga!

95 Eala þeodnes þrym!   Hu seo þrag gewat,
    genap under nihthelm,   swa heo no wære.
    Stondeð nu on laste   leofre duguþe
    weal wundrum heah,   wyrmlicum fah.
    Eorlas fornoman   asca þryþe,
100 wæpen wælgifru,   wyrd seo mære,
    ond þas stanhleoþu   stormas cnyssað,
    hrið hreosende   hrusan bindeð,
    wintres woma,   þonne won cymeð,
    nipeð nihtscua,   norþan onsendeð
105 hreo hæglfare   hæleþum on andan.
    Eall is earfoðlic   eorþan rice,
    onwendeð wyrda gesceaft   weoruld under heofonum.
    Her bið feoh læne,   her bið freond læne,
    her bið mon læne,   her bið mæg læne,
110 eal þis eorþan gesteal   idel weorþeð!"
        Swa cwæð snottor on mode,   gesæt him sundor æt rune.
    Til biþ se þe his treowe gehealdeþ,   ne sceal næfre his torn
                                        to rycene
    beorn of his breostum acyþan,   nemþe he ær þa bote
                                        cunne,
    eorl mid elne gefremman.   Wel bið þam þe him are seceð,
115 frofre to fæder on heofonum,   þær us eal seo fæstnung
                                        stondeð.

Acknowledgements

Thanks to the editors of the following publications who published previous versions of these poems and/or my poetry since the last book: *ARM: Academic Journal of Research on Mothering, Exile: The Literary Quarterly, LyricalMyrical Press, Qwerty, The New Quarterly, Variety Crossings, Zarez.* Thanks to Daniel Ehrenworth for using my works for *Holocaust Dream.* Thanks to Len Early, Gale Zoë Garnett, Erina Harris, David Lampe, and other writers and organizers for including me in so many events and/or teaching my work. Thanks as well to the hardworking translators for bringing some of my work to Korean, Croatian, and Latvian audiences, and to the fantastic Anglo-Saxon scholar, Dr. Antonette Di Paolo Healey, Director of the Dictionary of Old English (DOE) at the University of Toronto, for her very helpful suggestions and expert advice on "The Wanderer: A New Millennium Translation." And thanks to York University and the Division of Humanities for the continued support.

Thank you, as usual, to Barry Callaghan and Exile Editions. Thank you for all the dinners, drinks, writing stories, and nights of laughter. Thank you Claire, for you.

Thank you Richard Teleky for the long talks and our Tuesday night dinners. Thank you to Tim and Tracy and Babel Books, 123 Ossington, Toronto, the best used-book and vinyl record store in the city. Thanks to Halli & David for the trip to Detroit, and to Rishma Dunlop for Penticton. Thanks to all friends and family.

And, once again, all my love to Christopher Doda. Thank you for our house, our home, for taking care of me and the cats, for all the ways you make life worth living each and every day.

Exile Editions

info@exileeditions.com
www.ExileEditions.com

publishers of singular
fiction, poetry, drama, photography and art
since 1976